KINGFISHER
READERS

1

Brilliant Birds

Thea Feldman

KINGFISHER
NEW YORK

KINGFISHER
LONDON & NEW YORK

Copyright © Kingfisher 2015
Published in the United States by Kingfisher,
175 Fifth Ave., New York, NY 10010
Kingfisher is an imprint of Macmillan Children's Books, London.
All rights reserved.

Distributed in the U.S. and Canada by Macmillan,
175 Fifth Ave., New York, NY 10010

Library of Congress Cataloging-in-Publication data
has been applied for.

Series editor: Polly Goodman
Literacy consultant: Ellie Costa, Bank Street School for Children, New York

978-0-7534-7198-2 (HC)
978-0-7534-7199-9 (PB)

Kingfisher books are available for special
promotions and premiums. For details
contact: Special Markets Department,
Macmillan, 175 Fifth Ave., New York, NY 10010

For more information, please visit
www.kingfisherbooks.com

Printed in China
9 8 7 6 5 4 3 2 1
1TR/1014/WKT/UG/105MA

Picture credits
The Publisher would like to thank the following for permission to reproduce their material.
Every care has been taken to trace copyright holders. However, if there have been unintentional
omissions or failure to trace copyright holders, we apologize and will, if informed, endeavor to
make corrections in any future edition.
Top = t; Bottom = b; Center = c; Left = l; Right = r
Cover © Chris van Rijswijk/Minden Pictures/FLPA; Page 3 ZSSD/Minden Pictures/FLPA; 4 Shutterstock/
Menno Schaefer; 5 Shutterstock/Gerrit de Vries; 6 Shutterstock/Peter Krejzl; 7 © Frans Lanting/Corbis;
8 Frans Lanting/FLPA; 9 Keving Elsby/FLPA; 10 Marcel can Kammen/Minden Pictures/FLPA;
11 © Wayne Lynch/All Canada Photos/Corbis; 12 Shutterstock/Bonnie Taylor Barry; 13t Shutterstock/
Butterfly Hunter; 13b David Hosking/FLPA; 14 Erica Olsen/FLPA; 15 Shutterstock/Andre Valado;
16 Shutterstock/Maslov Dmitry; 17 © DLLILLC Corbis; 18 Shutterstock/Delmas Lehman; 19 Shutterstock
/nice_pictures; 20 Shutterstock/Peter van Graafelland; 21t Shutterstock/Chris T Pehlivan; 21b Donald
M. Jones/Minden Pictures/FLPA; 22 Stefan Hewiler/Naturepl; 23 Dietmar Nill/Naturepl; 24 Dave Watts/
Naturepl; 25 Phil Savoie/Naturepl; 26–27 Getty images/Kerstin Waurick; 28 Getty images/Kerstin
Waurick; 29 Getty images /Kerstin Waurick; 30l Shutterstock/Doug Lemke; 30r Shutterstock/Daniel
Herbert; 31 Shutterstock/Doug Lemke

Birds are in the sky.

Birds are in the water.

Birds are on the ground.

Birds are in trees.

Birds are even
in the coldest place
on Earth.

Birds are everywhere!

The ostrich is the biggest bird.

It is taller than
the tallest person!

It is much
heavier too.

The bee hummingbird
is the smallest bird.

actual size

It is smaller than
most butterflies.

It weighs less than
two paper clips!

What makes an
animal a bird?

Feathers!

Birds are the
only animals
that have feathers.

Birds have different
kinds of feathers.

Most birds have strong,
stiff feathers on their wings
and tails.

These feathers help birds fly.

Birds have soft
feathers.

These feathers
help a bird
stay warm.

Some birds have
very bright feathers.

Some birds have feathers in
colors that help them hide.

All birds have **wings.**

Most birds fly.

They use their wings to fly.

They spread their wings wide
and push up into the air.

Some birds that can fly
can swim too.

Webbed feet help them swim.

Some birds cannot fly.

Penguins are birds
that cannot fly.

Penguins use their wings
to swim!

Webbed feet help them
swim too.

Some birds fly away
when winter comes
each year.

They fly back in the spring.

The Arctic tern
can fly farther than
any other bird.

It flies more than 44,000 miles
(70,900 kilometers) round trip!

All birds have a **beak**.

A bird's beak is the right size
and the right shape
for the kind of food it eats.

This bird
eats insects.

This bird
eats seeds.

This bird catches fish
with its beak.

This bird
eats fruit.

This bird catches
and eats other animals.

When it is time to find a **mate**, most male birds try to get a female bird to notice them.

Some male birds dance to get noticed!

Some male birds
show their colors
to get noticed.

Every bird begins life
inside an egg.

Most mother birds lay eggs
in a **nest**.

After a few weeks,
the eggs **hatch**.

Most baby birds
are born without feathers.

They cannot see.

Their parents bring them food
and keep them warm.

When they are two weeks old, most baby birds have feathers and can see.

They are called **fledglings**.

When they are five weeks old, most birds are ready to learn how to fly.

They will soon be ready to leave the nest.

Birds are everywhere.

There may be birds
outside your window
right now.

Just take a look!

Glossary

beak the hard part of a bird's mouth

feathers thin coverings over a bird's body that keep it warm and dry. Feathers help a bird fly, hide, and find a mate.

fledglings young birds that are almost ready to fly

hatch to break out of an egg and be born

mate an animal partner; two mates have babies together

nest a home in which birds have their babies and raise them

webbed feet feet with a flap of skin between each toe

wings the parts of a bird's body that it uses to fly